Ultimate Power

Ultimate Power

by
Joanne Bunce

Christian Publishing Services, Inc.
Tulsa, Oklahoma

Ultimate Power
ISBN 0-88144-150-3
Copyright © 1990 by Joanne Bunce
Niagara Ministries
4430 Miller Road
Niagara Falls, New York 14304

Published by Christian Publishing Services, Inc.
P. O. Box 55388
Tulsa, Oklahoma 74155

Contents

Acknowledgment

My thanks, love, and appreciation to all those in my family and in the Body of Christ who have given and added so much to my life by their ongoing love and support as I "dig in" to the Word of God.

Introduction

A visit to see the young man who was to become my son-in-law was the reason I took five of my six children to Laredo, Texas, in January, 1973. Little did I know that this trip was to be the doorway to the path to God my heart had been seeking for nearly all of the years of my life.

As early as three years of age, my parents would find me with our huge family Bible stretched out across my little knees. Although I could not understand the Word, somehow I knew it was special for me.

Through the years, and through events that occurred prior to this Texas trip, the hunger for God's Word never grew weaker. In fact, that hunger simply became stronger. I had been born again early in 1973 and started a small Bible study in my home. Each Wednesday, a few ladies who shared my hunger would join me to drink coffee and study God's precious Word.

Our study had caused us to uncover promises and benefits in the Word that were supposed to belong to the people of God. However, we knew those blessings were not functioning in our own lives, and we began to ask God for them.

The trip to Texas was the first stop on the road to finding answers from God. On that visit, I experienced the event that must occur in every life if a person is to learn and grow in the Lord. I was baptized in the Holy Spirit.

In the following months, our 18-year-old daughter broke her back and was miraculously healed in two days. Weeks later, my husband, Ted, was totally restored after being burned with hydrofluoric acid in an industrial accident. Also, I was healed of a spine condition that had been slowly crippling me.

Yes, I met the power of God's living Word and His life in its fullest dimensions. The greatest marvel, perhaps, is that I had not been taught any special "formulas" or step-by-step operations of how to walk in the power of the Holy Spirit. I was shown the power of God simply because of His love and goodness.

How glorious it is to be able to share through His Word this wonderful power that I first saw in its Biblical setting. How glorious to know that I have been called to share with specific people assigned by God.

My only reason for writing this book is to share truths that I believe the Holy Spirit will use to cause faith, hope, and love to grow within all who read it and who are willing to be led by the Holy Spirit.

I pray that each reader will say, "Lead me, precious Holy Spirit, on my road to the fullness of all God wants me to be to me that He may be these things *through* me to touch others. Everywhere I go, I want there to be a demonstration of the fact that through all the people of God there is meant to be a release of His *ultimate power.*"

Significance of First Names

Did you ever wonder why God allowed so many verses of the Bible to be written that are nothing but lists of the *first* names of men and women of the past?

Notice that I said first names. Even today, these names are called "common" names.

Why are there no last names in Bible genealogies?

Even when family identity is being listed, only the father's first names are used. One of the profound things about the Bible is that people are known and recognized by their first names! This matter should not be passed over as being without major significance.

Have we for centuries passed over one of the greatest revelations of all the truths contained in the pages of God's Word? Have we passed by revelation that could once and for all put an end to prejudice and separation in the Body of Christ?

This is only one of the subjects we are going to look at in this book. I encourage you to spend much time considering what you read here and the scriptures that underlie the subjects discussed.

The Bible says we are the *habitation* (abode or house) of the Lord God, and as we go through these teachings, I would like you to see yourself as a carpenter. There are five blocks of building material in this book. Take these blocks and create in your thinking a picture of you, the builder, constructing yourself as God's house through the use of these blocks.

The Word teaches us that God dwelt on earth under the old covenant in a building — tent tabernacle or stone temple. However, the New Testament teaches us that *we* — born again believers — are the habitations of God. We must understand what kind of building God must have in which to dwell, then we will be able to properly build "houses" for God.

So, builder, get out your scriptural building tools; get in submission to the Teacher, the Holy Spirit; and find your instructional manual, the Word of God. Our faith assures us that the structure we build will be a house filled with *peace, power, and love.*

1
Building Block One:
The Answer to the Identity Crisis

In the beginning God... (Gen. 1:1).

A long time ago, I realized those four words were telling me that everything that exists comes from God. The Bible says that all things came into existence through Him.

> **All things were made and came into existence through Him; and without Him was not even one thing made that has come into being.**
>
> **John 1:3**

When I wrote *God's Faith Pattern*,[1] I shared the manufacturing concept. I said that, as faith is what pleases God, I know that with His Words and through faith He created everything that exists. When He had demonstrated the productive ability of His powers in creation, He gave those powers to man.

He built into His children His perfected power to create as He did and does. That is the way any good manufacturer does things, and all the more the way a good father does with his children.

If the people of God really knew what they possess and who they are, they would not be concerned about

---

[1]Bunce, Joanne. *God's Faith Pattern* (Niagara Falls: Niagara Ministries, 1982).

the devil. They would know that, by staying in faith, they would be in a position where he could not touch them. If indeed they knew who they are as sons of God, the devil could not do a thing to them.

The greatest need in the Church today, I believe, is for believers to know what a "true believer" is: someone who is *believing* all of the time. Some people do not realize that a *believer* always is supposed to be believing for something. It is a mistake to think that believers are resters.

While it is true that we are to enter a special place of rest in the Holy Spirit, this rest is a force of creative power, and it functions as *action through belief.*

> [The Father] has delivered and drawn us to Himself out of the control and the dominion of darkness and has transferred us into the kingdom of the Son of His love.
>
> **Colossians 1:13**

Like the Israelites who came out of Egypt and went into the Promised Land, we must go into a land where God will live in the midst of us.

Ever notice that in the middle of the night there are times when praise and worship will not really lift you up? Why is that? When that happens, it is because you are out of the "land of peace." The problems or thoughts in your mind are trying to make you think they are greater than the Word of God and your faith. However, as you make a commitment to rest on the Word, God Himself will lift you back to the place of peace.

The Word of God will keep you and give you peace. It will sustain you in the middle of the night, the middle of the day, or anytime. This is the working action of God's keeping peace. That same peace is a major key which works as we stay in the faith. As peace works, it causes the life of God to flow through us because of the blood.

That is the way we move through the process of restoration. Notice the Word says in Colossians 1:20:

> **And God purposed that through — by the service, the intervention of — Him (the Son) all things should be completely reconciled back to Himself, whether on earth or in heaven, as through Him [the Father] made peace by means of the blood of His cross.**

The Apostle Paul wrote that all things would be completely reconciled back to God. *Back* means that all things must return to a place where they once were. *Restoration* means things are not at this moment the way they used to be, but they are headed toward the place where one day they will be pure and perfect as in the beginning.

If I am going to restore anything, I have to know what it is going to be restored to — and therein lies the *number one block* upon which every foundation must be built: *knowing who you are in Christ*, knowing your identity.

The problem is that most Christians do not know how man is supposed to be, so how can they know what man needs to be restored to?

Religion — doctrines and traditions of men — have so watered down what man was created to be that the Church today dare not believe she is being restored to the position man shared with God originally. However, the Bible clearly reveals the relationship God and man shared in the beginning and *will* share as soon as the work of restoration is complete.

As we are the "buildings" under restoration, we need to look at the first building for a pattern that will help us as we are being rebuilt. Look at the very beginning of mankind, as Moses related the event in Genesis:

> **So God created man in His own image, in the image and likeness of God He created him; male and female He created them.**
>
> **Genesis 1:27**

> **Then the Lord God formed man of the dust of the ground, and breathed into his nostrils the breath or spirit of life; and man became a living being.**
>
> **Genesis 2:7**

The word *dust* used in this verse is the Hebrew word *aphar,* and it means "the tiniest, most minute particle."[2]

What is the tiniest single particle of anything? I am not going to talk about neutrons and protons, because I know they are tiny. However, they actually are part of the smallest particle of matter, which is the *atom.*

How strange that when Abraham was told his descendants would be as *aphar* (dust), that translators would later write in our Bible the *dust of the ground.* Why? Is it not possible that, without scientific knowledge of the atom, the tiniest particle that men could see and comprehend with their natural eyes, at the time those early scrolls were written, was the dust of the ground? Is it also possible that Adam's name was a description of what he actually was — an atom from the Author of all atoms?

---

[2]Blizzard, Dr. Roy. *Historical and Chronological Survey of the Old Testament Series.*

The next question is this: What power causes one small cell to grow into a fully developed human being? The answer is "the right environment, or atmosphere." What is the true fertile soil of God's life and garden? Is it not *faith*? By *faith*, God created everything that exists. (Heb. 11:3.) He is a *faith* God, and faith is how God created everything and caused everything to grow and develop.

Faith is "knowing that you know that you know." Hebrews 11:1 in *The Amplified Bible* says: **Faith is the assurance [the confirmation, the title-deed] of the things [we] hope for,** in other words, the absolute knowledge that what we speak forth will come to pass.

We know that the first man, Adam, fell from his position in God through disobedience. And, when Jesus was born, God was saying, "Here is the earthly form of Jehovah, and He *is* salvation. He is My Anointed One to reconcile the world to Myself. This is the One who is the reality of all the previous types and shadows."

When God wanted to seal His covenant with Abram, the man chosen by God to be the one through whom the Seed of Promise (Jesus) would be born, He gave Abram a *new name*. (Gen. 15.) God took Abram's natural name and placed in the middle of it an "h", making it *Abraham*. The "h" actually is the sound of the unutterable name of God Himself.

The name Abraham is the declaration of the fact that the natural (things of the physical world) has been blended with the spiritual (things of the supernatural world).

Forever gone was Abram, the name that was simply a description of a man with a physical identity.

This man had incorporated his identity with God's, and God had incorporated His identity with the man's. All that Abram had been was gone, and for all eternity, Abraham will be the name to identify the father of Israel, of Jesus, and of the Church.

When we enter into the covenant with God called "the new birth," physical life is transformed into the life of the spiritual realm, the life of God and two worlds become one. All of this is clearly laid out in names. Apparently, many Christians know that once they are born again, they have a place in two worlds — the natural and the supernatural. However, to the majority, this fact does not seem to be a reality.

Abraham continued in his natural life a long time — in terms of earth years — after he received God's name as part of his. Yet in the heavenlies, Abraham already had a life in God.

The power of the life of God being blended with the life of man, as proclaimed through the name exchanges in the Bible, has not been a revelation to most 20th century Christians. If there were a genuine understanding of the life blending of heaven and earth, there would not be so many hassles or misunderstandings in the Church about when a born again person *enters* the Kingdom of God.

God's name signifies the *totality* of all that He is, as there is a sense in which your name identifies the *totality* of all that you are. Once we understand all that is proclaimed and presented to us by God in the offering and presenting of His name to man, the real challenge is to overcome that limiting factor of the soul: the mind.

Surely as Moses stood before the burning bush and heard the name *I Am* for the first time, he must have faced the same challenge. God told Moses to use His name to identify Him to a people who as yet had no real knowledge of Him.

And God said to Moses, I AM WHO I AM and WHAT I AM, and I WILL BE WHAT I WILL BE; and He said, You shall say this to the Israelites, I AM has sent me to you . . . This is My name for ever, and by this name I am to be remembered to all generations.

Exodus 3:14,15b

The wonder of wonders is that *in Jesus Christ* we have been made with God the "I am's" of this world. As we declare according to the Word of God, "I am healed, I am redeemed, I am whole," and so forth, we actually are uniting earth to heaven. The words "I am" are declaring that God is *in you,* flowing and working through you, and that He is the totality of all you or anyone else will ever need.

The name Jews could not utter has become a part of our everyday way of identifying ourselves as the seeds and heirs of the one and only God through the real Seed of Promise, Jesus. Everytime you say, "I am a Christian," you are proclaiming a unity of all the power in both the natural and supernatural realms. You operate in both heaven and earth. That is why I am convinced that a major tactic of the forces of darkness has been, and is, to keep God's people from ever understanding name identification and the power associated with names.

Look again at those words, "According to the Word of God, *I am healed.*" What you are saying is: I AM, the heaven-side of the Word and life of God, and *healed* is the physical, earthly side of the creation of God which is in me. This is a true "power place." All of the banks of heaven will pay out a check or bank draft that has the *I AM* on it.

Jesus prayed, "Father, keep them through your name." (John 17:11.) How does the name of God keep us? *I AM* is the all-powerful name of God, and as I operate the declarations that are in line with His Word, I am being kept, for *I AM* keeps me.

No One Else Can Live Your 'Blueprint'

A name, then, carries a blueprint of a person just as a cell carries the full blueprint of all that its physical body will be in its fully developed state. Let us look at a New Testament example of the wonderful function of the naming process as seen in the story of Zacchaeus.

And when Jesus reached the place, He looked up and said to him, Zacchaeus, hurry and come down; for I must stay at your house today.

Luke 19:5

Jesus *stopped* under the tree where Zacchaeus was and called him by name. *Zacchaeus means "pure."*[3]

God was saying through His Son, "I *must*, I *need*, to go to your house today. You are not living up to your name, and I want to bring you to the point where you can express (identify) with your name."

Is it possible God had something to do with inspiring Zacchaeus's parents to name him as they did? God told Jeremiah that He knew and approved of him as a chosen instrument when He formed him in his mother's womb. (Jer. 1:5.)

---

[3]Packer, J. I.; Tenny, Merrill C.; White, William Jr. *The Bible Almanac* (Nashville: Thomas Nelson Publishers, 1980), p. 677.

One thing is certain: Zacchaeus might have been identified with the garbage of the world before Jesus came to his house, but once Jesus came, Zacchaeus experienced a complete housecleaning and became "pure." The Bible tells us that he was a "publican" by trade, a minor official who collected the tolls, or taxes, for transporting goods by land or by sea.[4]

The names of Adam, Abram, Jesus, and Zacchaeus are but a few examples of many in God's Word that are there to let us know something of the way God very specifically designed, built, and then set out to restore all of mankind who will allow Him to work in their lives.

The important point, the knowledge that can be a building block for you, is this:

Before the foundation of the earth, God made a blueprint for your life.

While not everyone fully lives God's exact blueprint, it is an attainable goal. It is possible. You must realize that you are not here by chance, nor are you an accident. You are part of the definite purpose set in motion by God. Not only did He name you, but He wrote your name over your job assignment and your position in the family of God. Usually, we refer to this "blueprint" as *your call.*

No one else can live *your* blueprint. Today, in some circles, we hear a lot about a theological principle that when God looks at us, He only sees Jesus. Yes, Jesus took the rags of our sin nature and gave us His robe of righteousness; and that means that I am now a

---

[4]Ibid, p. 529.

unique being who never existed before, and there is no one like me.

Lending yourself to the teaching and leading of the Holy Spirit will cause you to perform your mission on this earth, will allow you to live as the son or daughter of the *Great I AM* in the boldness in which you were created to live. If a majority of Christians would do this, I promise you the earth would never be the same, and Satan's kingdom would never be the same!

All of the names in the genealogies listed in the Bible were intended to tell later generations how unique that person was and what a special someone each one of us is.

Additional reading in the Word will seal this in your heart. Instead of skipping the genealogies as boring and useless, begin to study those names of unique people. Whether they fulfilled their true potential in God or not, they were designed to; for all are called, not by some chance accident but by direct appointment with God. However, the Word says few are chosen. (Matt. 20:16.) Only those who have come in line with the "call" on their lives, with the blueprint God designed for them, will answer the call.

With this as the first building block in our dwelling place, think of the house of power and glory each of us will be when we reach the last block!

God is the Creator and Giver of life, so the very fact that every man alive says "I am" many times during his lifetime is a declaration of the godly potential in each life. Needless to say, God intended this building block for man's upbuilding and betterment. We must be careful not to allow Satan to pervert that given by God.

The purpose and work of the Holy Spirit is to reveal the true *I AM* in anyone who is born of the spirit.

2
Building Block Two:
The Wisdom of God

The second building block is a much-needed thing in our lives and in the corporate Body of Christ, and that is *the wisdom of God*. As the Holy Spirit establishes the character of the Father in His children, He builds a foundation that must be solid in order for the life of God to securely and continually flow through a believer.

The psalmist wrote:

> **The reverent fear and worship of the Lord is the beginning of wisdom and skill [the preceding and the *first essential*, the prerequisite and the alphabet of them]. A good understanding, wisdom and meaning have all those who do [the will of the Lord]. Their praise of Him endures forever.**
>
> **Psalm 111:10**

The emphasis today on praise and worship is a clear declaration of where the Church is in this hour. The Holy Spirit has been teaching the Church true praise of God, a scriptural praise that will endure forever, a praise that cannot be shaken by anything. This praise is a proclamation that the Church is doing the will of God and doing it with the building tools of wisdom and skill.

In Luke 7:30-50, Jesus discussed the difference between spiritual and human wisdom. Look at verse 35:

> Yet wisdom is vindicated [shown to be true and divine] by all her children [that is, by their life, character, and deeds].

Obviously, the wisdom of God differs from the wisdom of men. Wisdom that men acquire through natural learning abilities is not truly wisdom but reason. Reason is a composite of the education received through the environment by the senses.

Human reason judges by surface things. Human reasoning believes that people who call themselves "believers" are because they act or react in a certain manner. Or they believe that because a certain voice inflection is used when praying, praising, or proclaiming God's Word, that person *really* knows God or is hearing from God.

Physical presentation or control is not necessarily a sign of spirituality. It may be a sign of religion, of ritualistic or programmed responses. True spirituality is proclaimed and displayed through the wisdom of God. This wisdom is the result of having settled the revelation of God's Word in your heart and in your life.

Human reasoning, if exalted over the wisdom of God, will result in spiritual death. If you reason away the things of God with your natural mind, you will never develop into a spiritually mature child of God. Real knowledge is the result of truth revealed to you by the Spirit of God and incorporated into your life by making your actions and behavior conform to that truth.

Wisdom can be defined as "the faculty of making the best use of knowledge."

The education you receive by the Spirit of God is eternal. This is true education. It does not set aside our natural abilities or faculties; it uses them for God's glory.

God's builders were men of wisdom. Wisdom was, and is, necessary equipment for those who build spiritual things. In Exodus 31:3, God said *wisdom* was one of the seven-fold characteristics of the Holy Spirit. God said He had filled the temple craftsman, Bezalel, with the Spirit of God to manifest in *wisdom* and ability, understanding, intelligence, knowledge, *and* all kinds of craftsmanship.

God's temple could not be built with only human reason and training. The temple was built by those operating in God's wisdom.

The Pathway to Wisdom

If you are a born again believer, filled with the Spirit of God, the potential for this wisdom to operate in your life is certain because it is *in* the Holy Spirit. Today, we are beholding God transforming *His true tabernacle,* His temple, with His wisdom-filled men and women.

The so-called restraints of human holiness never have, or never will, mature or develop the Christian believer into a blessed and glory-filled temple of God. Believers are temples with new hearts and natures attached to minds that are being renewed daily by God's Word. Individuals who are being brought into the true liberty of life in God. God's wisdom always has enveloped His people in His blessings and glory.

Revelation knowledge is the pathway that brings us to the door of wisdom; however, revelation is *not* wisdom. We will advance to the door of wisdom as we move in the action of the Word. Once we have revelation knowledge of portions of Scripture, it can never be taken from us but will lead us to be wise both in things of God and things of the earth.

Wisdom is the construction tool that will get you built into what God wants you to look like and eternally be.

> Bezalel and Aholiab and every wise-hearted man in whom the Lord has put wisdom and understanding to know how to do all the work for the service of the sanctuary, shall work according to all that the Lord has commanded.
>
> And Moses called Bezalel and Aholiab and every able and wise-hearted man in whose mind the Lord had put wisdom and ability, everyone whose heart stirred him up to come to do the work.
>
> Exodus 36:1,2

Building is work, and work can and does make us uncomfortable. Work is difficult at times. Again, these things can help us discern the times, for if ever the Church of the Lord Jesus Christ has appeared to be having some difficulties in uncomfortable places, today is the time.

In Scripture, the man functioning in the wisdom of God often did not function as someone operating with worldly knowledge might have. In fact, there are times when God's wisdom looks like foolishness. For example, no one with natural wisdom would have said to the women quarreling over a baby to cut the baby in half. (1 Kings 3:16-28.) Yet God's wisdom through Solomon caused the woman who was lying to be exposed.

> And all Israel heard of the judgment which the king had made, and they stood in awe of him, for they saw that the wisdom of God was in him, to do justice.
>
> 1 Kings 3:28

Wisdom Reveals the Purpose of the Blood

Psalm 51:7 points forward from King David's day to Calvary when the soldier put hyssop mixed with vinegar up to Jesus' mouth. (John 19:29.) Also, it points back to the time when bunches of hyssop dipped in blood were used to paint the doorways of the people of God during the Passover night in Egypt. (Ex. 12:6-13.)

> **Purify me with hyssop, and I shall be clean [ceremonially]; wash me, and I shall [in reality] be whiter than snow.**
>
> **Psalm 51:7**

Hyssop is a sweet-smelling bush of the mint family, and in Psalm 51, it is used by the psalmist as a symbol of inner cleansing. Some scholars think marjoram is what the Bible calls hyssop.[1] Marjoram is also of the mint family and has aromatic leaves. Hyssop, or any of the mint plants, smells sweet but tastes bitter.

Both examples of the use of hyssop are pictures of the same thing: the life in the blood covering others that death could pass over. The doorway to the true fullness of life and blessing in God is seeking His wisdom for understanding of the blood's effect and purpose in our lives.

Scripturally, the blood was applied through "the herb of bitterness," through being sprinkled over those things to be purified, and through things being dipped into the blood. (Ex. 12:22, Lev. 3:13, and many other verses.)

The seventh verse of Psalm 51 is in the context of, or tied to, the sixth verse which speaks of wisdom in

---

[1] *The Bible Almanac*, p. 252.

the inner man. Therefore, wisdom is the door to understand cleansing, or the purpose of the blood of Jesus, and is the answer to a hunger for truth.

Behold, you desire truth in the inner being, make me therefore to know wisdom in my inmost heart.
Psalm 51:6

If the Jewish people had operated in the wisdom of God instead of the knowledge of the religious leaders, they would never have doubted that Jesus was their long-awaited Savior. If they had hungered for truth and not knowledge, they would have had the desire of their innermost beings. In His life and in His death, all of the ceremonial rituals they observed for cleansing and purification were fulfilled. Somehow, however, they had never come to a realization that those rituals were symbols of the real Lamb and not fully effective in themselves.

Jesus fulfilled all of their feasts and every holy observance with His every action. He had the attitude of heart and did the works necessary to approach God in true righteousness. However, because the Jewish leaders of His day were controlled by their natural minds and their natural understanding of the Scripture, they lacked the wisdom that would have caused them to recognize their Redeemer.

They were well-educated in the Old Testament teachings, but in all cases, education must be submitted to the wisdom of the Holy Spirit. Education is necessary to live in today's world, but it cannot be *blended* with God's wisdom or *exalted* above it. It must be *submitted* to the Holy Spirit to give it spiritual understanding.

Knowledge gained through our natural educational processes changes almost daily in this Information Age. What was true yesterday may no longer be true tomorrow. Things in the scientific world that were considered absolutes yesterday are obsolete and discarded today. However, *God's wisdom never changes or varies.* It is ever the same.

> My son, if you will receive my words and treasure up my commandments with you,
>
> Making your ear attentive to skillful and godly Wisdom, and inclining and directing your heart and mind to understanding — applying all your powers to the quest for it;
>
> Yes, if you cry out for insight and raise your voice for understanding,
>
> If you seek Wisdom as silver, and search for skillful and godly Wisdom as for hid treasures;
>
> Then you will understand the reverent and worshipful fear of the Lord and find the knowledge of [our omniscient] God.
>
> **Proverbs 2:1-5**

It is necessary to apply all the power you have to the quest for the wisdom of God. That power is the might of the Holy Spirit. If He is in you, then you have the potential to be as wise as Solomon. In fact, you have the potential to be as wise as Jesus was when He walked on earth.

> For who has known or understood the mind (the counsels and purposes) of the Lord so as to guide and instruct [Him] and give Him knowledge? But *we have the mind of Christ,* the Messiah, and do hold the thoughts (feelings and purposes) of His heart.
>
> **1 Corinthians 2:16**

The wisdom of God will add to the length of your days:

> **Hear, O my son, and receive my sayings, and the years of your life shall be many.**
>
> Proverbs 4:10

If I hear and act on the Word of God, it is going to come to pass in and for me, for God swore by Himself and gave Himself to bring His Word to pass. With His own blood, He *guaranteed* that His Word will be fulfilled. If I lean on the wisdom of God and not on my own understanding, His promises will come true in My life.

> **Wisdom is as good as an inheritance, yes, more excellent it is for those [the living] who see the sun.**
>
> Ecclesiastes 17:11

Wisdom Grows and Increases

In Mark 6:2, we are told of a visit Jesus made to His hometown of Nazareth:

> **And on the Sabbath He began to teach in the synagogue; and many who listened to Him were utterly astonished, saying, Where did this [Man] acquire all this? What is the wisdom — the broad and full intelligence — [which has been] given to Him? What mighty works and exhibitions of power are wrought by His hands!**

Those questions are answered in Luke 2:40:

> **And the Child grew and became strong in spirit, filled with wisdom, and the grace (favor and spiritual blessing) of God was upon Him.**

Wisdom, then, is a growing and increasing thing developed by hearing and acting on the Word. That is why it is dangerous for people to become comfortable at a certain point of hearing and acting on the Word. What they do not realize is that there still is the potential to revert to the way of the flesh, and it is here that

Christians become carnal. They "sit down" spiritually and stop short of the progressive growth which becomes wisdom.

The Holy Spirit gave me a picture: He showed me a door then a highway. He said the *door* is the way we enter at the time we become new creatures, at the time we are born again. Then He told me that, after entering this door, we progress along the way of hearing and acting on the Word. He called it *the way of revelation*. Farther down the road, I saw a second door, and it was labeled wisdom.

Revelation _____ **Wisdom.**

The Holy Spirit also showed me that the entrance to this second door, Wisdom, was covered with the works of the flesh, with carnality. He showed me that those works and all of their pressures were to be dealt with before entering. Revelation knowledge of the Word of God brings forth these carnal things from hidden places in a believer's life. If the believer will then give up those things and allow the Holy Spirit to cleanse them away under the blood of Jesus, that believer will advance into the fullness of the abundant life of God.

The first doorway is the place where many Christians today are finding themselves: Revelation but not yet wisdom.

How often have you seen someone with the Word of God in his life — even revelation of that Word — fall through some carnal action that seems so foolish? The person yielded to the carnality rather than moving it aside to advance through the doorway. Those who already have advanced through the way of wisdom must pray and release the weaker ones in order for them to see their own responses. They too can be led to change their ways and come on through the door of wisdom to experience the blessings and glory that lies just beyond.

> **But they were not able to resist the intelligence and the wisdom and [the inspiration of] the Spirit with which he spoke.**
>
> **Acts 6:10**

This verse tells us that when we are moving and acting by the Spirit of God, being led by His wisdom, people will be unable to resist us, unable to stand against, or refute what we say. That is why there is so much satanic opposition to our attempts to gain access to the door of wisdom.

If you are asking, "Is wisdom operating my life," I would in turn ask you these questions:

*What degree of power do you experience in your daily life?

*Have you come to the place where you do not strive to get the benefits of the Christian life, but rather, do you know by revelation those blessings are yours?

*Do you want to share your revelation with others?

If you can answer positively to these three questions, then wisdom is in operation in your life. You have passed through the door, and now it is your task to bring others through the same door.

3

Building Block Three:
An Understanding of Eternal Life

One of the major reasons there are so many defeated, lukewarm Christians is that they do not have a clear understanding of eternal life. To say, "I have been born again," is not an end in itself. That is like having someone hand you a bank book with the statement that a sum of money has been deposited in this account for you — but when you open the book, you cannot find the deposit entry! There is a major missing factor, and that deposit is the factor that will enable you to use what you have received.

The factor that will enable us to understand everything we have become and everything we have in Christ is to catch a glimpse of what *eternal life* means.

Because there is so much flesh-consciousness, or carnality, in the Church today, it is of vital importance that Christians come to the realization of what eternal life involves. If the Church is to stop being dependent on feelings and human reason and grow up, she must see where she is going.

How can we tell that the Church, in general, has remained at such an infant stage?

Look at the biggest selling books and the most popular teachings. They are those that cover emotional, fleshly activities with a thin layer of spiritual principles.

Certainly there is a sense in which the activities performed by spiritual beings are spiritual because of the one doing them. However, that does not make the activity itself spiritual. True spirituality must originate with God.

For example, ask anyone what he thinks heaven will be like, and his response will more than likely be a myriad of emotional answers, most of them based on an escapist mentality. "Getting away from it all" has a lot to do with why many Christians want to go to heaven. I have big news for them: That is not a true revelation of eternal life.

Adherents of some other religions, such as Islam, believe that if they "grin and bear it" here on earth, they will be able to experience the full release of their emotional, and even sensual, desires in the after life. However, that should not be the Christian view.

[The Father] has delivered and drawn us to Himself out of the control and the dominion of darkness and has transferred us into the kingdom of the Son of His love.

Colossians 1:13

For [as far as this world is concerned] you have died, and your [new, real] life is hid with Christ in God.

Colossians 3:3

Notice that a believer enters eternal life when he is born again, and he can begin to enjoy eternal life even while he is still on earth in the flesh.

Eternal Life Is an Absence of Time

The only way I, or any believer, can understand that eternal life is a place where there are no clocks or calendars is through the Word of God. *The Word of God is the only eternal thing I can touch while in this physical body.* Therefore eternal life to me is the Word, which has become the real life to and through my physical body.

True life is God's life. His Word is His life, so there are no alternatives or options. To be born of God means to be born of His Spirit, and the Bible is the description of how spirit beings live, now and forevermore. Satan will do everything he can to keep us from understanding that.

In the only two places in the Bible where it is recorded that Satan spoke, you will notice that he quoted the Word.

When he spoke to Eve in Genesis 3, he questioned God's word, but he quoted it. In Luke 4, when he offered Jesus the kingdoms of this world to keep Him from continuing to establish God's kingdom on earth, Satan quoted verses from the Old Testament to Jesus.

Since Satan's only real power is somehow to deceive, he must set out to deceive the Church in a way that appears like truth. He must appear as an angel of light. You cannot counterfeit what does not exist.

The building block which must rest firmly on the first two is the fact that you know eternal life is not so much what you are *getting* as it is *appropriating* that which you already have and will always have forever and ever.

4
Building Block Four: God Among the Animals, or The True Mark of the Beast

Every year as the Christmas season approaches, in Christian homes and offices alike, plans get under way to display the nativity. The birth of Jesus is the center of all this season proclaims, although most of the secular world tries to ignore that fact.

Of course, a nativity display is incomplete without several animals gathered around the principal characters. At least, that is the way the Church has imagined the event for almost two thousand years. Most Christians know by now that the "stable of the inn" was not a building such as we have today, but most likely a cave common to the part of the world where Jesus was born.

The focus of this building block is the nativity scene, or rather, some questions about that scene:

*Was it necessary that there be animals surrounding Jesus' birthplace?

*Was God's place among the animals a one-time occurrence, or was that a picture, a type, of something that still occurs?

> **And God said, Let the earth bring forth living creatures according to their kinds: livestock, creeping**

things, and [wild] beasts of the earth according to their kinds. And it was so.

Genesis 1:24

God made the animals *and* man on the same day, the sixth day of Creation. He said **let the earth bring forth** so we see the earth had the ability to produce, as did man.

It is important for us to remember that God is an ever-creating Being and that all things He creates are made with the ability to re-create (reproduce) after their own kind.

Then the Lord God formed man of the dust of the ground, and breathed into his nostrils the breath or spirit of life; and man became a living being.

Genesis 2:7

Then God breathed His *breath* into the man formed of the earth. Herein is the major difference between man and animal. This difference is the most vital thing man must learn. The breath of God and the similarity to the image of God clearly are what separates two kinds of fleshly creatures.

According to Genesis 2:7, animals were living creatures but obviously did not have the same kind of life which man received through the breath of God. From the beginning, we see there are two forms of life, and man alone received the life breath of God.

Adam's power and authority on earth, which separated him from all other things created by God, had to be entwined with the special life breath he received during his creation. Man had superiority on the earth. Why? He was superior because of his God-breathed life which was demonstrated through his authority and through his ability to do what God alone can do, create through his spoken word what is in his mind.

> And the Lord God took the man and put him in the Garden of Eden to tend and guard and keep it.
>
> And the Lord God commanded the man, saying, You may freely eat of every tree of the garden,
>
> Except of the tree of the knowledge of good and evil and of blessing and calamity you shall not eat, for in the day that you eat of it you shall surely die.
>
> Now the Lord God said, It is not good [sufficient, satisfactory] that the man should be alone; I will make him a helper meet (suitable, adapted, completing) for him.
>
> And out of the ground the Lord God formed every [wild] beast and living creature of the field and every bird of the air, and brought them to Adam to see what he would call them; and whatever Adam called every living creature, that was its name.
>
> And Adam gave names to all livestock, and to the birds of the air, and to every [wild] beast of the field; but for Adam there was not found a helper meet (suitable, adapted, completing) for him.
>
> **Genesis 2:15-20**

In these verses, we see two of the abilities mentioned above: Adam spoke forth the names he had created. Herein is great superiority and authority over the animal kingdom demonstrated. Animals may be trained to mimic people, but they do not and cannot create words.

What a wondrous thing it is to recall the precious times we have viewed this powerful operation in the life of a child. There is a very real way in which everything changes for a child once he speaks intelligible words. When a child is learning to speak, he is beginning to utilize the equipment which dictates almost totally the lifestyle in which he will function — not just on earth but in eternity. His words are the proclamation of his present living condition and the establishment of his future.

Creativity, however, cannot be limited to physical reproduction. There is another entirely different sense of creativity. Reproduction is a *natural* creative ability, a biological function. However, true *creativity* is vested in the power of the tongue. (Prov. 18:21.)

When Adam and Eve sinned, they lost their communion with God; the life of God departed from them, and they became spiritually separated from God, which is the true meaning of death: separation from God.

When man lost the breath, or the *zoe* life of God, what actually separated him from the beastly class? Was it simply his mind, his body structure, and the ability of physical speech? I say "physical speech" because *as long as man was of God, his words were not simply physical words.* When Adam spoke in the Garden during those days of innocence, his words were as God's Words, and God's Words are spirit and life.

From Genesis 3 on, we begin to see that once the life of God departed, and man's words became simply those of a physical man, Satan began to work to eradicate from earth everything else that was of God. He had been given authority over man by Adam and Eve. The devil immediately began to pervert or destroy everything that resembled God in man's mind, speech, and flesh. It is through these members that man displays the nature of his master.

In a strange way, *under Satan's authority,* man began to take on *an almost animalistic nature and appearance.* Man, the one created in the God-class of being, began to look and even sound like an animal.

By the time Jesus was born, whole groups or nations were being called "dogs" and "pigs." The animal identity began to replace man-created-in-the-image-of-God.

The *True* Mark of the Beast

I know you have seen people, maybe even been one in some way, a human who resembles one less than human. God could not be seen through your dress; the places you went, you did not think God would go; what you watched on television, God would not view; nor was God heard in your speech. Yes, there has been on some and remains on many today the true *mark of the beast* — man unable to live the life that is the only *real* life there is, the life we call "the abundant life."

Satan's plan and all of his works endeavor to make man remain in the animal class, causing man to think and act as an animal. Animals use others and allow themselves to be used and abused. For, after all, is that not what animals were created for — to be under authority, serve, and give pleasure? Thinking like an animal, I use another and move on because that person is really nothing but another animal, and we do not expect anything godly from animals.

By the time Jesus came to earth, man was living and functioning at a level so far below God's original plan for him (but remember the good news of the nativity), God came among the animals to restore man, to lift him out of death into life once again, with the position and authority in which he was originally created to function.

An interesting Bible-study project is to look up all the other scriptures where God is revealed among the animals. In the Old Testament, there are a number of places where God likens man to this or that animal. These places where we see man with an animal identity paint very graphic pictures. Jesus used the same pictures, such as admonishing His disciples that He was sending them out as "sheep" among "wolves" and to be "wise as serpents" and "harmelss as doves" (Matt. 10:16.)

Animals in the Covenant of Abraham

In Genesis 15:9-12, Abram brought animals to offer as part of the covenant God was about to make with him. This covenant described in detail in Genesis, chapters 15 and 17 served to blend two non-related people; to, in essence, make them one. The new covenant, made by Jesus with man, is the reality of which other covenants were pictures.

> **And he said to him, Bring to Me a heifer three years old, a she-goat three years old, a ram three years old, a turtledove, and a young pigeon.**
>
> **And he brought Him all these, and cut them down the middle (into halves) and laid each half opposite the other; but the birds he did not divide.**
>
> **And when the birds of prey swooped down upon the carcasses, Abram drove them away.**
>
> **When the sun was setting a deep sleep overcame Abram, and a horror, (a terror, a shuddering fear), of great darkness assailed and oppressed him.**
>
> **Genesis 15:9-12**

> When the sun had gone down and a (thick)
> darkness had come on, lo, a smoking oven and a
> flaming torch passed between those pieces.

> On the same day the Lord made a covenant
> (promise, pledge) with Abram, saying, To your
> descendants I have given this land, from the river of
> Egypt to the great river Euphrates.

Genesis 15:17,18

Of all the prayers I have for the Body of Christ, my greatest is that they would see the visual truths in the actions described in Genesis 15 and receive a personal identification with what occurred when Abram and God "cut covenant."

Abram presented and prepared the flesh and the animal blood, then dropped down in the midst of the blood life of the animals. From the heavenlies, this picture is just the way man appeared before God at that point in time because of the separation of sin: man as one dead in animal life. Animal life was all Abram had to bring to God.

But what did God bring to this covenant? Praise the Lord that each partner to a covenant brings himself! Abram brought himself, and God came to identify Himself with mankind.

What did man lack and need so desperately after the first couple was driven from the Garden of Eden? He needed spiritual life, a re-identification with God, through atonement for sin.

In verse 17, we read that God in a tangible form walked through the halved carcasses and through the blood of the animals, the substances Abram had sunk into. *God intermingled His life with the life in the flesh and blood of animal creation.* God, who *is* life, walked through that maze of animal flesh.

Here the Word proclaims that the living God entered into covenant with the man Abram, thus affecting all of Abram's descendants, natural and spiritual. *The animal life of man was blended with and came upon God as he walked through the blood,* and the life of flesh which no longer had a spirit life, received the life of God and God would appear after this time as the Lamb.

In Genesis 22:8, a powerful statement is made as Abraham is walking up Mount Moriah with his beloved son, Isaac, who asked, **Father, where is the lamb?" Abraham answered, "God will provide Himself the lamb." (Gen. 22:7,8).** That, of course, is another picture for us. Was not God the lamb of the new covenant sacrifice? Yes, God provided Himself as the Lamb. What is a lamb but an animal?

There is a sense in which, through the covenant with Abram, God entered into the flesh (the animal life) of man that had remained on earth after Adam sinned.

When God came at the nativity, His identification with man's physical, as well as spiritual, condition fulfilled a picture shown two thousand years before in the Abrahamic covenant. At His birth, the Seed of God *and* Abraham was in that manger. The conception of Jesus actually began in Genesis 15. When Abram rose from that blood and flesh laid out on the ground, he was no longer representative of spiritually empty mankind for by faith he saw the day man would live *zoe* life again.

The living Word of God had been imparted to flesh. When Abram came up out of that place of identification with God, he had a whole new life. So, too, God — the Word — had taken upon Himself flesh.

If God were going to deliver man and bring him out of his sin, animal life, and restore man to Himself as a Bride, He had to become like him. God's first law expressed in the earth is for "like to mate with and reproduce with one like himself." Each different species of plant or animal life was to reproduce with his own kind. One statute given to the Israelites through Moses was not to mate different kinds of animals or races. (Lev. 19:19.)

At the nativity, we see the beginning of God's actual lifting of man out of animal identification in order that those who love and serve Him might be on the throne of the universe with the God-Man, Jesus Christ, the throne that the Lamb (animal) brought the blood of God to, as we can see in Revelation 4. Yes, the Lamb slain became the King Lord.

Reminders of the God-Man Identification

Throughout the Old Testament, we can see the reminders of the transference of identification between flesh life and spirit life. In Leviticus 17:11, the Lord told Moses that life was in the blood.

> **For the life (the animal soul) is in the blood, and I have given it for you upon the altar to make atonement for your souls; for it is the blood that makes atonement, by reason of the life [which it represents].**

So surely when men shed the blood of animals, it represented the flesh-life of man. Then God received that life, taking it unto Himself and sanctifying it with His own life.

Consider the tabernacle in the wilderness, where God dwelt among men. Everything in the tabernacle proclaimed and displayed God's dwelling place. Once a year, the high priest took the animal blood into the tabernacle through the first door. Then he proceeded past the light, the bread of life, and the altar of incense through the second doorway into the actual place where the blood was placed on the piece of furniture called "the mercy seat." (Lev. 16.)

This seat covered the Ark of the Covenant, and the Ark contained three items that revealed all that God-Among-Man would be: the Word (scrolls of God's laws), the priesthood (Aaron's rod that budded), and manna (the bread of life that contains miracle-working power).

The mercy seat is a reminder of Genesis 15 where God took upon Himself animal life and also a foreshadowing of the nativity scene. If you are ever to really understand redemption, identification power, and the authority of Jesus, you must see its beginning in the Abrahamic covenant. Blood is everything to life. Remember: life and *all* it represents is in the blood.

We can see in the spoils of war in the Old Testament that the victor would capture *man and beast*. Truly, for a season after the Edenic "battle" for Adam and Eve's souls, the enemy captured man and beasts. However, God already had made a plan to rectify the defeat. Jesus Christ is the **lamb slain before the foundation of the world** (1 Pet. 1:20).

Satan may have received man and beast as his spoils temporarily, but the war did not end there. That was just the beginning skirmish. You and I live today after the main battle, Calvary, and we are on the side of victory!

Yes, Satan still has men "marked" with beast life, and he uses tools that were meant to be used by the sons of God. The *mouth* is the tool of creating, the decreeing, proclaiming tool. But the *mind* is the instrument that goes to work the minute words are spoken to produce the fruit, the reality, of those words.

Satan has set out to use television, the printed page, and everything else on which he can get his hands to mark the minds of men. Those marked men then contaminate the lives of anyone and everyone they encounter through their speech and through their flesh.

Jesus was born on earth among animals so that all who would see or hear would remember how God's identification with all men began when He originally covenanted with the man Abraham.

This is to remind you that if you have accepted Jesus as your personal Savior, you have been sealed by His Holy Spirit in a new birth. You have become a new species, a new class of being. (2 Cor. 5:17.) You have received a very true, very real, blood-life identification with God.

As you read and study the Word, your flesh is being transformed to experience the restoration to the resemblance of the God to whom you were engrafted through the new birth. The "animal life" is leaving, and the godly nature is working its way through you. No longer are you a "666" man. You are a Christian, a "little

Christ," a whole new type of being. In Jesus Christ, you have moved into an entirely new kingdom.

In the fall of Adam, man died to the abilities that are God's and began to live in an animal class. However, Jesus came to earth to lie in a manger amongst the animals. And, in the second Adam, we have received the life-giving Spirit of the Almighty God.

To be without Christ is to be as Mephibosheth, Jonathan's only living son, who called himself when speaking to David — "a dead dog" (2 Sam. 9:8). However, to be in Christ is to be in another totally separate class, the God-life class. Can you see why all the forces of hell are aligned to keep man from knowing and living in this knowledge which clearly reveals what kingdom redeemed man has been transferred into by Jesus Christ?

We could spend so much more space developing this lesson! We could go to Daniel and see how King Nebuchadnezzar became as an animal, and there are many other places that reveal the difference between the old, animal nature and the new God-nature. If you are born again, I want to exhort you to stand tall as the Christ-man the nativity and cross made you to be, a member of the new species.

5

Building Block Five:
Desperate Faith

The fifth building block is *desperate faith*. I believe God is saying to the Body of Christ that now is the time to get desperate, or perhaps we could say, to get *violent*, because Jesus said the violent take the Kingdom by force. (Matt. 11:12.)

Look at the Canaanite woman who came to Jesus *desperate* over her demon-possessed daughter. (Matt. 15.) True desperation brought her to the feet of Jesus, and she was determined to allow nothing or no one to discourage or hinder her. Desperation fans a determination that will not give up.

My prayer is that the Holy Spirit will make each reader *desperate through identification with this Canaanite woman*. She came to see Jesus because she had heard of a Man who was setting captives free. I pray her story will motivate you to action, so that your life will reach those God means for you to set free as you live in this freedom.

Desperate faith will lead you to a broader fuller knowledge that gives you the ability to get anyone free. This involves one of the most attacked messages of our day — the kingdom message. Understanding of this message is directly connected with the Canaanite woman and her success in receiving from Jesus.

The Canaanite woman did not have a clouded view of the Kingdom of God, although apparently some Jews did — in spite of the fact that Jesus was displaying God's Kingdom right before their eyes. One of the real issues in Matthew 15 is: Where is the Kingdom?

> **And going away from there, Jesus withdrew to the district of Tyre and Sidon.**
>
> **And behold, a woman who was a Canaanite of that district came out and with a (loud, troublesomely urgent) cry begged, Have mercy on me, O Lord, Son of David! My daughter is miserably and distressingly and cruelly possessed by a demon!**
>
> **But He did not answer her a word. And His disciples came and implored Him, saying, Send her away, for she is crying after us.**
>
> **He answered, I was sent only to the lost sheep of the house of Israel.**
>
> **But she came and kneeling, worshipped Him, and kept praying, Lord, help me!**
>
> **And He answered, It is not right — proper, becoming or fair — to take the children's bread and throw it to the little dogs.**
>
> **She said, Yes, Lord, yet even the little pups eat the crumbs that fall from their (young) masters' table.**
>
> **Then Jesus answered her, O woman, great is your faith! Be it done for you as you wish. And her daughter was cured from that moment.**
>
> **Matthew 15:21-28**

Before this incident, Jesus already had said that He was the Bread of Life. (John 6.) It is a simple conclusion to assume then that when I receive the Bread, Jesus, I also receive the Kingdom. Bread is a natural substance, yet God used it to demonstrate the natural blending with the supernatural. When Jesus said that He was the Bread and that healing is the children's bread, He was giving supernatural life to apparently natural substance.

The mercy for which this woman came to Jesus was supernatural power. Obviously, many people around this woman and her daughter had pity on them, but pity alone is a natural emotion, definitely not enough to get anyone healed. Jesus, the New Kingdom man, was the constant picture of the union of the natural and spiritual *which is what the Kingdom of God is all about.*

Desperation Knows No Obstacles

The first thing we see in this event is that the woman was a *Canaanite.* When you see certain national names in the Bible, there should be an understanding that a certain culture and lifestyle is associated with that name. If you have read the Bible any time at all, and you see *Canaanite,* the word that goes with it is "dog."

The Jewish people considered the Canaanite people the scum of the earth, people who only knew darkness. They were "a lower class," a people that the chosen of God never went near. They were "untouchables."

And the Canaanite woman knew what the attitude of the Jews would be to her. However, desperation will cause a person to pass over anything that looks like an obstacle if a place of receiving, or a place of help, exists beyond that obstacle.

So she approached Jesus with a *troublesome, urgent cry* and begged His mercy on her. How could she dare to do such a thing? She simply had the nerve and boldness of desperation, which pays no attention to things such as social standing, race, sex, or national barriers. Her situation was akin to the lepers of Jesus day who were required to cry, "Unclean, unclean," to anyone who came near.

She might as well have been a leper! How dared a Canaanite, *and* a woman at that, come near to a Jewish rabbi (teacher)? Yet, because of her desperation, what others called her meant nothing. The fact that she was forbidden to be there meant nothing. She might as well be dead anyhow, so what could they do to her?

When people came to Jesus calling Him "Son of David," that meant they acknowledged His kingly lineage and were looking for the kind of mercy only a king can grant, which is *a pardon*. In granting her pardon, there is a sense in which she actually would be removed from the penalty of sin. When calling on David's line, the woman actually was setting herself and her family in submission to true royalty, to the highest authority.

She was acknowledging Jesus as royalty when even those who were closest to Him — His own disciples — had not yet understood His real identity. They did not believe He was royalty in the natural, much less in the Kingdom of God.

The fullness of truth that Jesus brought to earth was once again a reuniting of natural and supernatural royalty and authority. What else is a kingdom? However, *the Jews were looking for an earthly warrior to conquer the earth, not a God-man Messiah.*

The Canaanite woman knew the key to the deliverance her child needed: mercy. If there is a King who can grant me a pardon that will remove the sin of any nationality into which I was born, then this pardon also can remove me from everything else that separates me from what is good.

Then the woman became specific. Her daughter was miserably and distressingly and cruelly possessed by a demon.

What was the disciples' reaction? As men who had given up all to follow Jesus, surely they were looking for people who could be helped. How could they be following Jesus and not be looking for troubled, tormented people? They could follow Him and not look for hurting people to point to Him the same way we do today — through looking at those around us with blinded spiritual eyes.

When Jesus pointed out the difference in nationalities to her, He really was notifying her of the change of identity that must take place, if she were going to receive what she sought. Only when you release your strongholds of race, nationality, gender, and class, can you begin to understand the true Kingdom of God.

If Jesus is King, then let us demonstrate His Kingdom in the same way He did: by granting mercy and pardon. If His Word and the pattern of His life are my guides, then His mercy and pardon are so strong that captives will be set free regardless of their national origin.

As the woman received her daughter's deliverance, she began to worship Jesus. Worship is the surrender, the yielding of all you are, physically and spiritually. Worship is a cleansing, restoring acknowledgment that

Jesus is Lord. Therefore, her worship became the establishment of the Kingdom of David, at least to her.

This woman knew enough to know that *on this earth* there was to be a demonstration of the Kingdom of One whose pardon, because of His mercy, would enable her daughter to be released from demonic possession immediately.

All over the world today are people like the disciples. They go around proclaiming themselves the people of God, yet they deny and miss the real truth of Who He is that is proclaimed and displayed through the Word. How many people really worshiped Jesus while He was on earth? Only a few, among them we find Mary who washed His feet with her hair, and a blind man. However the tragedy is that the list of worshipers would not include those who knew Him well *until after His death*.

How many of those around Jesus should have been making desperate demands on behalf of those bound by demons or afflicted with infirmities? Yet, like many today, His closest disciples were not desperate but seemed focused on their personal needs or on the prestige of following a teacher of national fame.

I would rather be found among those who say Jesus is King, who determine Him to be established *now* as King in every situation where His power and authority is needed.

The Heart of Kingdom Thinking

The heart of Kingdom thinking, then, becomes a changing of focus from oneself to others who need to be freed or healed. Oh, God of King David's line and before, *be King!*

The attack upon Christians who believe that they are already in the Kingdom of God has puzzled many. The "Kingdom reality" is a simple Bible truth which was the center of the full plan of redemption, for Jesus cannot be King (Lord) over your life if you are not *in* His Kingdom. Eternal life is *now* for those who have accepted Jesus as Savior.

Have you ever wondered why there are no surnames, no last names, in the Bible? Why did the Holy Spirit go to such great lengths to include many lines which have never really seemed to say much to us? The answer is because those lines are the key of all keys, the proclamation of all proclamations.

Those names with no surnames, those first names with no last names, reveal the total of all that life in God is about. *In Him there is the only nationality that is true nationality.* (2 Cor. 5:17.)

What makes a Christian? According to Second Corinthians 5:17, a Christian is a totally new creature because of identification with the blood of Jesus. Remember that Leviticus 17:11 says the life *and all it represents* is in the blood.

That means that, in Jesus Christ, I am a new creature and a member of a *new nation.* Nationality is determined by bloodlines. The Bible is the Book of the Blood. It tells us of the way God made, through faith, to get His godly bloodline restored to mankind on earth.

I like pizza, spaghetti, and Italian foods. I have been to Rome, and I even have the foundation of a fairly good Italian name. However, I am not born of Italian lineage, therefore I can never be Italian. Nationality is a sure, sealed, unchangeable fact because of the witness of the blood. Since the blood inheritance factor is in the father, we can say your blood tells clearly who your father is.

I am certain last names were not used in Bible times, because God knew the day would come when the second Adam would come to earth with the first name of Jesus.

Jesus was crucified and resurrected by the power of the Word of God. He applied His blood on the mercy seat, blood which brought the eternal nationality of mankind (all who will receive it) into reality once again.

Today, our Lord is not just a man named *Jesus*. He is Jesus Christ. We are Christians, or "little Christs." The nationality of God is sure in the earth and heavenlies today, for this truly is eternal life. We are people who have found a Kingdom whose Ruler and Maker is God.

Does that mean we no longer have a regard for the Jewish people? No, it does not. I praise God for them and love them. After all, in Jesus Christ, we are one. But God cannot have a divided Kingdom. Jesus said a kingdom divided against itself will fall. (Mark 3:24,25.) Why will such a conflict cause something to fall? The reason is that a division, a fracture, weakens anything. It is not solid any longer.

It is past time for the Church to move into the true unity which Jesus died for us to know. Every time the national or racial blood in a human's veins is exalted over one's supernatural identity, the blood of Jesus is set aside as inferior to the blood of mankind. Either there is *one* nation in God, and the blood of Jesus is the source of our lives, or what was done at Calvary did not do a total and complete job of making a people for God.

We cannot separate our understanding of true nationality from our understanding of the Kingdom. Whenever Satan moves in the Church to cloud a relatively simply spiritual truth, you better believe there is a need for grasping that truth in a desperate way! We need to hold to it desperately because the enemy is trying to steal it from us.

Concerning the Kingdom of God and the controversy that has arisen about it, we should understand that all of the noise and furor means Satan is trying to obscure or steal a truth from the Church. That particular fact, or truth, must be extremely important for the Church to understand or the enemy would not be trying so hard to cover it up or pervert it.

If we do not know God must have a Kingdom, how can we truly come under His leadership to receive the title and covenant rights as kings that rule and reign under His dominion and authority? The issue of the Kingdom is very important, for without a settled understanding of the simple basics of this message, there is no way we can properly exercise our spiritual authority.

Satan was defeated at the cross, yet demon authority has never appeared to have a greater stronghold on earth over the lives of those whose only hope is God's Kingdom! The primary reason for understanding the Kingdom and where it exists is so that we can bring others into it. How can people come to a Kingdom if they do not know where it is?

The Canaanite woman did not have the clouded view of the Kingdom.

My challenge to you, dear reader, is not to relegate to "someday," to "pie in the sky by and by" what is so desperately needed today. Leave the hassling over theology to those who do not have family or friends who need deliverance or healing or salvation. As for me, I am looking for the desperate. Please join me. Come and be desperate with me!

Desperate faith will get the demon-possessed free.

A Final Word

I could give you a *whole stack* of building blocks and all the tools to build a "house," but if you never start to work, obviously you will never have a house. I believe the Church today is separated from the abundant life promised in the Word because of Christians' neglecting to appropriate that life. No one informed of an enormous earthly inheritance would neglect to claim it. No, that person would hasten immediately to get hold of what was his.

Yet, despite the years of teaching in very exact definite ways about how to possess and live the abundant life, there is still far too much lack in the Body of Christ. In service after service, I hear people asking the Lord to do what He *has* already done. It is not "majoring on minors" to tell Christians to find out what Jesus did for us on the cross, then begin to live out that benefit in their lives.

This lack of living out what has been accomplished makes God's people a "set up" for every sensational ministry that comes down the road and for every trick of the devil. Once and for all, we must decide to live out of our inheritance and not out of our old fleshly responses, thoughts, and preferences.

Maturity is on the verge of bursting forth in every part of the Church, and it will, through those who have recognized and received new life from the Word.

We are not just going to have eternal life in the hereafter, but we have eternal life in the here and now. Implicit in the word *eternal* is the meaning "outside of time" or "separated from time."

Please do not just read about these "building blocks," but accept them, integrate them into your life, and begin to act on them. I am *desperate* for your health and deliverance. This is a book of desperate faith on your behalf.